MY HEALTHY LIFE JOURNAL

MY HEALTHY LIFE JOURNAL

DAILY WRITING TO CREATE INTENTION AND AWARENESS WITH YOUR HEALTH AND WELL-BEING

Jenn Benson

ISBN: 0996484221
ISBN 13: 9780996484220

This journal belongs to: _____

If found, please contact me at: _____

Dedicated to everyone and anyone who wants to make healthy changes and live with intention. You are smart and amazing people. YOU CAN DO IT!

Hello, and thanks for picking up this journal. My guess is that you are in need of some healthy changes and you are looking for a way to get started. Well, big pat on the back and a double high five. You are in the right place! This journal is a simple start to building attention and awareness to your habits. Once you can identify habits and focus on the positive changes you are making on a daily basis, you will soar above and be completely unstoppable. Sometimes we just need one simple focus that will propel us forward to a happy, healthier life. The act of writing consistently will bring about changes you didn't even see coming! It isn't complicated, but it's effective.

HOW TO USE THIS JOURNAL

Start your morning with the first question *I woke up grateful for...* This sets the tone for the day in an empowering and positive light. It makes sense then, to end your day just before bedtime by filling out the rest of the journal. This allows you to reflect on the day and all of those positive choices you made to better your health and well-being. It's a true snapshot and over time, you can look back, notice patterns, and have a complete timeline in chronological order of the memories and events that lead to your amazing life. Be sure to use the blank pages in the back for notes and new discoveries. *"Writing is the painting of the voice"* *~ Voltaire.*

Living with awareness and intention is true freedom. You are in fact, what you believe you are and you will be, in fact what you believe you will be. Create the life of your dreams. Start writing, start simple, just start!

Love, Jenn ♥

Please be sure to visit me online at www.jennbenson.com for more resources and to say hello!

Date   /   /

I woke up grateful for

_____

_____

The best part of my day was

_____

_____

My healthy habit of the day was

_____

_____

The healthy food I chose to nourish my body was

_____

_____

The amount of water I drank was

_____

_____

My active movement of the day was

_____

_____

My overall feeling and mood of the day was

_____

_____

I reduced my stress by

_____

_____

I am going to bed grateful for

_____

_____

Date   /   /

I woke up grateful for

_____

_____

The best part of my day was

_____

_____

My healthy habit of the day was

_____

_____

The healthy food I chose to nourish my body was

_____

_____

The amount of water I drank was

_____

_____

My active movement of the day was

_____

_____

My overall feeling and mood of the day was

_____

_____

I reduced my stress by

_____

_____

I am going to bed grateful for

_____

_____

Date   /   /

I woke up grateful for
_____

_____

The best part of my day was
_____

_____

My healthy habit of the day was
_____

_____

The healthy food I chose to nourish my body was
_____

_____

The amount of water I drank was
_____

_____

My active movement of the day was
_____

_____

My overall feeling and mood of the day was
_____

_____

I reduced my stress by
_____

_____

I am going to bed grateful for
_____

_____

Date / /

I woke up grateful for
_____

_____

The best part of my day was
_____

_____

My healthy habit of the day was
_____

_____

The healthy food I chose to nourish my body was
_____

_____

The amount of water I drank was
_____

_____

My active movement of the day was
_____

_____

My overall feeling and mood of the day was
_____

_____

I reduced my stress by
_____

_____

I am going to bed grateful for
_____

_____

Date   /   /

I woke up grateful for
_____
_____

The best part of my day was
_____
_____

My healthy habit of the day was
_____
_____

The healthy food I chose to nourish my body was
_____
_____

The amount of water I drank was
_____
_____

My active movement of the day was
_____
_____

My overall feeling and mood of the day was
_____
_____

I reduced my stress by
_____
_____

I am going to bed grateful for
_____
_____

Date / /

I woke up grateful for

_____

_____

The best part of my day was

_____

_____

My healthy habit of the day was

_____

_____

The healthy food I chose to nourish my body was

_____

_____

The amount of water I drank was

_____

_____

My active movement of the day was

_____

_____

My overall feeling and mood of the day was

_____

_____

I reduced my stress by

_____

_____

I am going to bed grateful for

_____

_____

Date   /   /

I woke up grateful for
_____
_____

The best part of my day was
_____
_____

My healthy habit of the day was
_____
_____

The healthy food I chose to nourish my body was
_____
_____

The amount of water I drank was
_____
_____

My active movement of the day was
_____
_____

My overall feeling and mood of the day was
_____
_____

I reduced my stress by
_____
_____

I am going to bed grateful for
_____
_____

Date / /

I woke up grateful for

_____

_____

The best part of my day was

_____

_____

My healthy habit of the day was

_____

_____

The healthy food I chose to nourish my body was

_____

_____

The amount of water I drank was

_____

_____

My active movement of the day was

_____

_____

My overall feeling and mood of the day was

_____

_____

I reduced my stress by

_____

_____

I am going to bed grateful for

_____

_____

Date   /   /

I woke up grateful for
_____

_____

The best part of my day was
_____

_____

My healthy habit of the day was
_____

_____

The healthy food I chose to nourish my body was
_____

_____

The amount of water I drank was
_____

_____

My active movement of the day was
_____

_____

My overall feeling and mood of the day was
_____

_____

I reduced my stress by
_____

_____

I am going to bed grateful for
_____

_____

Date   /   /

I woke up grateful for
_____
_____

The best part of my day was
_____
_____

My healthy habit of the day was
_____
_____

The healthy food I chose to nourish my body was
_____
_____

The amount of water I drank was
_____
_____

My active movement of the day was
_____
_____

My overall feeling and mood of the day was
_____
_____

I reduced my stress by
_____
_____

I am going to bed grateful for
_____
_____

Date   /   /

I woke up grateful for
_____
_____

The best part of my day was
_____
_____

My healthy habit of the day was
_____
_____

The healthy food I chose to nourish my body was
_____
_____

The amount of water I drank was
_____
_____

My active movement of the day was
_____
_____

My overall feeling and mood of the day was
_____
_____

I reduced my stress by
_____
_____

I am going to bed grateful for
_____
_____

Date / /

I woke up grateful for

_____

_____

The best part of my day was

_____

_____

My healthy habit of the day was

_____

_____

The healthy food I chose to nourish my body was

_____

_____

The amount of water I drank was

_____

_____

My active movement of the day was

_____

_____

My overall feeling and mood of the day was

_____

_____

I reduced my stress by

_____

_____

I am going to bed grateful for

_____

_____

Date   /   /

I woke up grateful for

_____

_____

The best part of my day was

_____

_____

My healthy habit of the day was

_____

_____

The healthy food I chose to nourish my body was

_____

_____

The amount of water I drank was

_____

_____

My active movement of the day was

_____

_____

My overall feeling and mood of the day was

_____

_____

I reduced my stress by

_____

_____

I am going to bed grateful for

_____

_____

Date   /   /

I woke up grateful for

_____

_____

The best part of my day was

_____

_____

My healthy habit of the day was

_____

_____

The healthy food I chose to nourish my body was

_____

_____

The amount of water I drank was

_____

_____

My active movement of the day was

_____

_____

My overall feeling and mood of the day was

_____

_____

I reduced my stress by

_____

_____

I am going to bed grateful for

_____

_____

Date   /   /

I woke up grateful for
_____
_____

The best part of my day was
_____
_____

My healthy habit of the day was
_____
_____

The healthy food I chose to nourish my body was
_____
_____

The amount of water I drank was
_____
_____

My active movement of the day was
_____
_____

My overall feeling and mood of the day was
_____
_____

I reduced my stress by
_____
_____

I am going to bed grateful for
_____
_____

Date / /

I woke up grateful for

_____

_____

The best part of my day was

_____

_____

My healthy habit of the day was

_____

_____

The healthy food I chose to nourish my body was

_____

_____

The amount of water I drank was

_____

_____

My active movement of the day was

_____

_____

My overall feeling and mood of the day was

_____

_____

I reduced my stress by

_____

_____

I am going to bed grateful for

_____

_____

Date   /   /

I woke up grateful for
_____
_____

The best part of my day was
_____
_____

My healthy habit of the day was
_____
_____

The healthy food I chose to nourish my body was
_____
_____

The amount of water I drank was
_____
_____

My active movement of the day was
_____
_____

My overall feeling and mood of the day was
_____
_____

I reduced my stress by
_____
_____

I am going to bed grateful for
_____
_____

Date / /

I woke up grateful for

_____

_____

The best part of my day was

_____

_____

My healthy habit of the day was

_____

_____

The healthy food I chose to nourish my body was

_____

_____

The amount of water I drank was

_____

_____

My active movement of the day was

_____

_____

My overall feeling and mood of the day was

_____

_____

I reduced my stress by

_____

_____

I am going to bed grateful for

_____

_____

Date   /   /

I woke up grateful for

_____

_____

The best part of my day was

_____

_____

My healthy habit of the day was

_____

_____

The healthy food I chose to nourish my body was

_____

_____

The amount of water I drank was

_____

_____

My active movement of the day was

_____

_____

My overall feeling and mood of the day was

_____

_____

I reduced my stress by

_____

_____

I am going to bed grateful for

_____

_____

Date / /

I woke up grateful for

_____

_____

The best part of my day was

_____

_____

My healthy habit of the day was

_____

_____

The healthy food I chose to nourish my body was

_____

_____

The amount of water I drank was

_____

_____

My active movement of the day was

_____

_____

My overall feeling and mood of the day was

_____

_____

I reduced my stress by

_____

_____

I am going to bed grateful for

_____

_____

Date   /   /

I woke up grateful for

_____

_____

The best part of my day was

_____

_____

My healthy habit of the day was

_____

_____

The healthy food I chose to nourish my body was

_____

_____

The amount of water I drank was

_____

_____

My active movement of the day was

_____

_____

My overall feeling and mood of the day was

_____

_____

I reduced my stress by

_____

_____

I am going to bed grateful for

_____

_____

Date   /   /

I woke up grateful for

_____

_____

The best part of my day was

_____

_____

My healthy habit of the day was

_____

_____

The healthy food I chose to nourish my body was

_____

_____

The amount of water I drank was

_____

_____

My active movement of the day was

_____

_____

My overall feeling and mood of the day was

_____

_____

I reduced my stress by

_____

_____

I am going to bed grateful for

_____

_____

Date   /   /

I woke up grateful for
_____
_____

The best part of my day was
_____
_____

My healthy habit of the day was
_____
_____

The healthy food I chose to nourish my body was
_____
_____

The amount of water I drank was
_____
_____

My active movement of the day was
_____
_____

My overall feeling and mood of the day was
_____
_____

I reduced my stress by
_____
_____

I am going to bed grateful for
_____
_____

Date / /

I woke up grateful for
_____
_____

The best part of my day was
_____
_____

My healthy habit of the day was
_____
_____

The healthy food I chose to nourish my body was
_____
_____

The amount of water I drank was
_____
_____

My active movement of the day was
_____
_____

My overall feeling and mood of the day was
_____
_____

I reduced my stress by
_____
_____

I am going to bed grateful for
_____
_____

Date   /   /

I woke up grateful for

_____

_____

The best part of my day was

_____

_____

My healthy habit of the day was

_____

_____

The healthy food I chose to nourish my body was

_____

_____

The amount of water I drank was

_____

_____

My active movement of the day was

_____

_____

My overall feeling and mood of the day was

_____

_____

I reduced my stress by

_____

_____

I am going to bed grateful for

_____

_____

Date   /   /

I woke up grateful for

_____

_____

The best part of my day was

_____

_____

My healthy habit of the day was

_____

_____

The healthy food I chose to nourish my body was

_____

_____

The amount of water I drank was

_____

_____

My active movement of the day was

_____

_____

My overall feeling and mood of the day was

_____

_____

I reduced my stress by

_____

_____

I am going to bed grateful for

_____

_____

Date   /   /

I woke up grateful for

_____

_____

The best part of my day was

_____

_____

My healthy habit of the day was

_____

_____

The healthy food I chose to nourish my body was

_____

_____

The amount of water I drank was

_____

_____

My active movement of the day was

_____

_____

My overall feeling and mood of the day was

_____

_____

I reduced my stress by

_____

_____

I am going to bed grateful for

_____

_____

Date   /   /

I woke up grateful for
_____
_____

The best part of my day was
_____
_____

My healthy habit of the day was
_____
_____

The healthy food I chose to nourish my body was
_____
_____

The amount of water I drank was
_____
_____

My active movement of the day was
_____
_____

My overall feeling and mood of the day was
_____
_____

I reduced my stress by
_____
_____

I am going to bed grateful for
_____
_____

Date   /   /

I woke up grateful for

_____

_____

The best part of my day was

_____

_____

My healthy habit of the day was

_____

_____

The healthy food I chose to nourish my body was

_____

_____

The amount of water I drank was

_____

_____

My active movement of the day was

_____

_____

My overall feeling and mood of the day was

_____

_____

I reduced my stress by

_____

_____

I am going to bed grateful for

_____

_____

Date   /   /

I woke up grateful for
_____

_____

The best part of my day was
_____

_____

My healthy habit of the day was
_____

_____

The healthy food I chose to nourish my body was
_____

_____

The amount of water I drank was
_____

_____

My active movement of the day was
_____

_____

My overall feeling and mood of the day was
_____

_____

I reduced my stress by
_____

_____

I am going to bed grateful for
_____

_____

Date   /   /

I woke up grateful for

_____

_____

The best part of my day was

_____

_____

My healthy habit of the day was

_____

_____

The healthy food I chose to nourish my body was

_____

_____

The amount of water I drank was

_____

_____

My active movement of the day was

_____

_____

My overall feeling and mood of the day was

_____

_____

I reduced my stress by

_____

_____

I am going to bed grateful for

_____

_____

Date   /   /

I woke up grateful for
_____
_____

The best part of my day was
_____

My healthy habit of the day was
_____
_____

The healthy food I chose to nourish my body was
_____
_____

The amount of water I drank was
_____
_____

My active movement of the day was
_____
_____

My overall feeling and mood of the day was
_____
_____

I reduced my stress by
_____
_____

I am going to bed grateful for
_____
_____

Date   /   /

I woke up grateful for
_____
_____

The best part of my day was
_____
_____

My healthy habit of the day was
_____
_____

The healthy food I chose to nourish my body was
_____
_____

The amount of water I drank was
_____
_____

My active movement of the day was
_____
_____

My overall feeling and mood of the day was
_____
_____

I reduced my stress by
_____
_____

I am going to bed grateful for
_____
_____

Date / /

I woke up grateful for

_____

_____

The best part of my day was

_____

_____

My healthy habit of the day was

_____

_____

The healthy food I chose to nourish my body was

_____

_____

The amount of water I drank was

_____

_____

My active movement of the day was

_____

_____

My overall feeling and mood of the day was

_____

_____

I reduced my stress by

_____

_____

I am going to bed grateful for

_____

_____

Date / /

I woke up grateful for

_____

_____

The best part of my day was

_____

_____

My healthy habit of the day was

_____

_____

The healthy food I chose to nourish my body was

_____

_____

The amount of water I drank was

_____

_____

My active movement of the day was

_____

_____

My overall feeling and mood of the day was

_____

_____

I reduced my stress by

_____

_____

I am going to bed grateful for

_____

_____

Date   /   /

I woke up grateful for

_____

_____

The best part of my day was

_____

_____

My healthy habit of the day was

_____

_____

The healthy food I chose to nourish my body was

_____

_____

The amount of water I drank was

_____

_____

My active movement of the day was

_____

_____

My overall feeling and mood of the day was

_____

_____

I reduced my stress by

_____

_____

I am going to bed grateful for

_____

_____

Date   /   /

I woke up grateful for
_____
_____

The best part of my day was
_____
_____

My healthy habit of the day was
_____
_____

The healthy food I chose to nourish my body was
_____
_____

The amount of water I drank was
_____
_____

My active movement of the day was
_____
_____

My overall feeling and mood of the day was
_____
_____

I reduced my stress by
_____
_____

I am going to bed grateful for
_____
_____

Date   /   /

I woke up grateful for

_____

_____

The best part of my day was

_____

_____

My healthy habit of the day was

_____

_____

The healthy food I chose to nourish my body was

_____

_____

The amount of water I drank was

_____

_____

My active movement of the day was

_____

_____

My overall feeling and mood of the day was

_____

_____

I reduced my stress by

_____

_____

I am going to bed grateful for

_____

_____

Date   /   /

I woke up grateful for
_____
_____

The best part of my day was
_____
_____

My healthy habit of the day was
_____
_____

The healthy food I chose to nourish my body was
_____
_____

The amount of water I drank was
_____
_____

My active movement of the day was
_____
_____

My overall feeling and mood of the day was
_____
_____

I reduced my stress by
_____
_____

I am going to bed grateful for
_____
_____

Date / /

I woke up grateful for

_____

_____

The best part of my day was

_____

_____

My healthy habit of the day was

_____

_____

The healthy food I chose to nourish my body was

_____

_____

The amount of water I drank was

_____

_____

My active movement of the day was

_____

_____

My overall feeling and mood of the day was

_____

_____

I reduced my stress by

_____

_____

I am going to bed grateful for

_____

_____

Date / /

I woke up grateful for

_____

_____

The best part of my day was

_____

_____

My healthy habit of the day was

_____

_____

The healthy food I chose to nourish my body was

_____

_____

The amount of water I drank was

_____

_____

My active movement of the day was

_____

_____

My overall feeling and mood of the day was

_____

_____

I reduced my stress by

_____

_____

I am going to bed grateful for

_____

_____

Date   /   /

I woke up grateful for
_____
_____

The best part of my day was
_____
_____

My healthy habit of the day was
_____
_____

The healthy food I chose to nourish my body was
_____
_____

The amount of water I drank was
_____
_____

My active movement of the day was
_____
_____

My overall feeling and mood of the day was
_____
_____

I reduced my stress by
_____
_____

I am going to bed grateful for
_____
_____

Date / /

I woke up grateful for
_____
_____

The best part of my day was
_____
_____

My healthy habit of the day was
_____
_____

The healthy food I chose to nourish my body was
_____
_____

The amount of water I drank was
_____
_____

My active movement of the day was
_____
_____

My overall feeling and mood of the day was
_____
_____

I reduced my stress by
_____
_____

I am going to bed grateful for
_____
_____

Date   /   /

I woke up grateful for

_____

_____

The best part of my day was

_____

_____

My healthy habit of the day was

_____

_____

The healthy food I chose to nourish my body was

_____

_____

The amount of water I drank was

_____

_____

My active movement of the day was

_____

_____

My overall feeling and mood of the day was

_____

_____

I reduced my stress by

_____

_____

I am going to bed grateful for

_____

_____

Date   /   /

I woke up grateful for
_____
_____

The best part of my day was
_____
_____

My healthy habit of the day was
_____
_____

The healthy food I chose to nourish my body was
_____
_____

The amount of water I drank was
_____
_____

My active movement of the day was
_____
_____

My overall feeling and mood of the day was
_____
_____

I reduced my stress by
_____
_____

I am going to bed grateful for
_____
_____

Date   /   /

I woke up grateful for

_____

_____

The best part of my day was

_____

_____

My healthy habit of the day was

_____

_____

The healthy food I chose to nourish my body was

_____

_____

The amount of water I drank was

_____

_____

My active movement of the day was

_____

_____

My overall feeling and mood of the day was

_____

_____

I reduced my stress by

_____

_____

I am going to bed grateful for

_____

_____

Date / /

I woke up grateful for

_____

_____

The best part of my day was

_____

_____

My healthy habit of the day was

_____

_____

The healthy food I chose to nourish my body was

_____

_____

The amount of water I drank was

_____

_____

My active movement of the day was

_____

_____

My overall feeling and mood of the day was

_____

_____

I reduced my stress by

_____

_____

I am going to bed grateful for

_____

_____

Date   /   /

I woke up grateful for

_____

_____

The best part of my day was

_____

_____

My healthy habit of the day was

_____

_____

The healthy food I chose to nourish my body was

_____

_____

The amount of water I drank was

_____

_____

My active movement of the day was

_____

_____

My overall feeling and mood of the day was

_____

_____

I reduced my stress by

_____

_____

I am going to bed grateful for

_____

_____

Date   /   /

I woke up grateful for
_____
_____

The best part of my day was
_____
_____

My healthy habit of the day was
_____
_____

The healthy food I chose to nourish my body was
_____
_____

The amount of water I drank was
_____
_____

My active movement of the day was
_____
_____

My overall feeling and mood of the day was
_____
_____

I reduced my stress by
_____
_____

I am going to bed grateful for
_____
_____

Date   /   /

I woke up grateful for
_____
_____

The best part of my day was
_____
_____

My healthy habit of the day was
_____
_____

The healthy food I chose to nourish my body was
_____
_____

The amount of water I drank was
_____
_____

My active movement of the day was
_____
_____

My overall feeling and mood of the day was
_____
_____

I reduced my stress by
_____
_____

I am going to bed grateful for
_____
_____

Date   /   /

I woke up grateful for
_____
_____

The best part of my day was
_____
_____

My healthy habit of the day was
_____
_____

The healthy food I chose to nourish my body was
_____
_____

The amount of water I drank was
_____
_____

My active movement of the day was
_____
_____

My overall feeling and mood of the day was
_____
_____

I reduced my stress by
_____
_____

I am going to bed grateful for
_____
_____

Date   /   /

I woke up grateful for
_____

_____

The best part of my day was
_____

_____

My healthy habit of the day was
_____

_____

The healthy food I chose to nourish my body was
_____

_____

The amount of water I drank was
_____

_____

My active movement of the day was
_____

_____

My overall feeling and mood of the day was
_____

_____

I reduced my stress by
_____

_____

I am going to bed grateful for
_____

_____

Date   /   /

I woke up grateful for
_____
_____

The best part of my day was
_____
_____

My healthy habit of the day was
_____
_____

The healthy food I chose to nourish my body was
_____
_____

The amount of water I drank was
_____
_____

My active movement of the day was
_____
_____

My overall feeling and mood of the day was
_____
_____

I reduced my stress by
_____
_____

I am going to bed grateful for
_____
_____

Date   /   /

I woke up grateful for

_____

_____

The best part of my day was

_____

_____

My healthy habit of the day was

_____

_____

The healthy food I chose to nourish my body was

_____

_____

The amount of water I drank was

_____

_____

My active movement of the day was

_____

_____

My overall feeling and mood of the day was

_____

_____

I reduced my stress by

_____

_____

I am going to bed grateful for

_____

_____

Date   /   /

I woke up grateful for
_____
_____

The best part of my day was
_____
_____

My healthy habit of the day was
_____
_____

The healthy food I chose to nourish my body was
_____
_____

The amount of water I drank was
_____
_____

My active movement of the day was
_____
_____

My overall feeling and mood of the day was
_____
_____

I reduced my stress by
_____
_____

I am going to bed grateful for
_____
_____

Date   /   /

I woke up grateful for

_____

_____

The best part of my day was

_____

_____

My healthy habit of the day was

_____

_____

The healthy food I chose to nourish my body was

_____

_____

The amount of water I drank was

_____

_____

My active movement of the day was

_____

_____

My overall feeling and mood of the day was

_____

_____

I reduced my stress by

_____

_____

I am going to bed grateful for

_____

_____

Date / /

I woke up grateful for

_____

_____

The best part of my day was

_____

_____

My healthy habit of the day was

_____

_____

The healthy food I chose to nourish my body was

_____

_____

The amount of water I drank was

_____

_____

My active movement of the day was

_____

_____

My overall feeling and mood of the day was

_____

_____

I reduced my stress by

_____

_____

I am going to bed grateful for

_____

_____

Date / /

I woke up grateful for

_____

_____

The best part of my day was

_____

_____

My healthy habit of the day was

_____

_____

The healthy food I chose to nourish my body was

_____

_____

The amount of water I drank was

_____

_____

My active movement of the day was

_____

_____

My overall feeling and mood of the day was

_____

_____

I reduced my stress by

_____

_____

I am going to bed grateful for

_____

_____

Date   /   /

I woke up grateful for

_____

_____

The best part of my day was

_____

_____

My healthy habit of the day was

_____

_____

The healthy food I chose to nourish my body was

_____

_____

The amount of water I drank was

_____

_____

My active movement of the day was

_____

_____

My overall feeling and mood of the day was

_____

_____

I reduced my stress by

_____

_____

I am going to bed grateful for

_____

_____

Date   /   /

I woke up grateful for

_____

_____

The best part of my day was

_____

_____

My healthy habit of the day was

_____

_____

The healthy food I chose to nourish my body was

_____

_____

The amount of water I drank was

_____

_____

My active movement of the day was

_____

_____

My overall feeling and mood of the day was

_____

_____

I reduced my stress by

_____

_____

I am going to bed grateful for

_____

_____

Date / /

I woke up grateful for
_____
_____

The best part of my day was
_____
_____

My healthy habit of the day was
_____
_____

The healthy food I chose to nourish my body was
_____
_____

The amount of water I drank was
_____
_____

My active movement of the day was
_____
_____

My overall feeling and mood of the day was
_____
_____

I reduced my stress by
_____
_____

I am going to bed grateful for
_____
_____

Date   /   /

I woke up grateful for

_____

_____

The best part of my day was

_____

_____

My healthy habit of the day was

_____

_____

The healthy food I chose to nourish my body was

_____

_____

The amount of water I drank was

_____

_____

My active movement of the day was

_____

_____

My overall feeling and mood of the day was

_____

_____

I reduced my stress by

_____

_____

I am going to bed grateful for

_____

_____

Date   /   /

I woke up grateful for
_____
_____

The best part of my day was
_____
_____

My healthy habit of the day was
_____
_____

The healthy food I chose to nourish my body was
_____
_____

The amount of water I drank was
_____
_____

My active movement of the day was
_____
_____

My overall feeling and mood of the day was
_____
_____

I reduced my stress by
_____
_____

I am going to bed grateful for
_____
_____

Date   /   /

I woke up grateful for

_____

_____

The best part of my day was

_____

_____

My healthy habit of the day was

_____

_____

The healthy food I chose to nourish my body was

_____

_____

The amount of water I drank was

_____

_____

My active movement of the day was

_____

_____

My overall feeling and mood of the day was

_____

_____

I reduced my stress by

_____

_____

I am going to bed grateful for

_____

_____

Date   /   /

I woke up grateful for

_____

_____

The best part of my day was

_____

_____

My healthy habit of the day was

_____

_____

The healthy food I chose to nourish my body was

_____

_____

The amount of water I drank was

_____

_____

My active movement of the day was

_____

_____

My overall feeling and mood of the day was

_____

_____

I reduced my stress by

_____

_____

I am going to bed grateful for

_____

_____

Date / /

I woke up grateful for
_____
_____

The best part of my day was
_____
_____

My healthy habit of the day was
_____
_____

The healthy food I chose to nourish my body was
_____
_____

The amount of water I drank was
_____
_____

My active movement of the day was
_____
_____

My overall feeling and mood of the day was
_____
_____

I reduced my stress by
_____
_____

I am going to bed grateful for
_____
_____

Date   /   /

I woke up grateful for
_____
_____

The best part of my day was
_____
_____

My healthy habit of the day was
_____
_____

The healthy food I chose to nourish my body was
_____
_____

The amount of water I drank was
_____
_____

My active movement of the day was
_____
_____

My overall feeling and mood of the day was
_____
_____

I reduced my stress by
_____
_____

I am going to bed grateful for
_____
_____

Date   /   /

I woke up grateful for

_____

_____

The best part of my day was

_____

_____

My healthy habit of the day was

_____

_____

The healthy food I chose to nourish my body was

_____

_____

The amount of water I drank was

_____

_____

My active movement of the day was

_____

_____

My overall feeling and mood of the day was

_____

_____

I reduced my stress by

_____

_____

I am going to bed grateful for

_____

_____

Date   /   /

I woke up grateful for

_____

_____

The best part of my day was

_____

_____

My healthy habit of the day was

_____

_____

The healthy food I chose to nourish my body was

_____

_____

The amount of water I drank was

_____

_____

My active movement of the day was

_____

_____

My overall feeling and mood of the day was

_____

_____

I reduced my stress by

_____

_____

I am going to bed grateful for

_____

_____

Date / /

I woke up grateful for

_____

_____

The best part of my day was

_____

_____

My healthy habit of the day was

_____

_____

The healthy food I chose to nourish my body was

_____

_____

The amount of water I drank was

_____

_____

My active movement of the day was

_____

_____

My overall feeling and mood of the day was

_____

_____

I reduced my stress by

_____

_____

I am going to bed grateful for

_____

_____

Date   /   /

I woke up grateful for
_____
_____

The best part of my day was
_____
_____

My healthy habit of the day was
_____
_____

The healthy food I chose to nourish my body was
_____
_____

The amount of water I drank was
_____
_____

My active movement of the day was
_____
_____

My overall feeling and mood of the day was
_____
_____

I reduced my stress by
_____
_____

I am going to bed grateful for
_____
_____

Date   /   /

I woke up grateful for

_____

_____

The best part of my day was

_____

_____

My healthy habit of the day was

_____

_____

The healthy food I chose to nourish my body was

_____

_____

The amount of water I drank was

_____

_____

My active movement of the day was

_____

_____

My overall feeling and mood of the day was

_____

_____

I reduced my stress by

_____

_____

I am going to bed grateful for

_____

_____

Date   /   /

I woke up grateful for

_____

_____

The best part of my day was

_____

_____

My healthy habit of the day was

_____

_____

The healthy food I chose to nourish my body was

_____

_____

The amount of water I drank was

_____

_____

My active movement of the day was

_____

_____

My overall feeling and mood of the day was

_____

_____

I reduced my stress by

_____

_____

I am going to bed grateful for

_____

_____

Date   /   /

I woke up grateful for

_____

_____

The best part of my day was

_____

_____

My healthy habit of the day was

_____

_____

The healthy food I chose to nourish my body was

_____

_____

The amount of water I drank was

_____

_____

My active movement of the day was

_____

_____

My overall feeling and mood of the day was

_____

_____

I reduced my stress by

_____

_____

I am going to bed grateful for

_____

_____

Date   /   /

I woke up grateful for
_____
_____

The best part of my day was
_____
_____

My healthy habit of the day was
_____
_____

The healthy food I chose to nourish my body was
_____
_____

The amount of water I drank was
_____
_____

My active movement of the day was
_____
_____

My overall feeling and mood of the day was
_____
_____

I reduced my stress by
_____
_____

I am going to bed grateful for
_____
_____

Date   /   /

I woke up grateful for

_____

_____

The best part of my day was

_____

_____

My healthy habit of the day was

_____

_____

The healthy food I chose to nourish my body was

_____

_____

The amount of water I drank was

_____

_____

My active movement of the day was

_____

_____

My overall feeling and mood of the day was

_____

_____

I reduced my stress by

_____

_____

I am going to bed grateful for

_____

_____

Date   /   /

I woke up grateful for
_____
_____

The best part of my day was
_____
_____

My healthy habit of the day was
_____
_____

The healthy food I chose to nourish my body was
_____
_____

The amount of water I drank was
_____
_____

My active movement of the day was
_____
_____

My overall feeling and mood of the day was
_____
_____

I reduced my stress by
_____
_____

I am going to bed grateful for
_____
_____

Date   /   /

I woke up grateful for

_____

_____

The best part of my day was

_____

_____

My healthy habit of the day was

_____

_____

The healthy food I chose to nourish my body was

_____

_____

The amount of water I drank was

_____

_____

My active movement of the day was

_____

_____

My overall feeling and mood of the day was

_____

_____

I reduced my stress by

_____

_____

I am going to bed grateful for

_____

_____

Date / /

I woke up grateful for

_____

_____

The best part of my day was

_____

_____

My healthy habit of the day was

_____

_____

The healthy food I chose to nourish my body was

_____

_____

The amount of water I drank was

_____

_____

My active movement of the day was

_____

_____

My overall feeling and mood of the day was

_____

_____

I reduced my stress by

_____

_____

I am going to bed grateful for

_____

_____

Date   /   /

I woke up grateful for

_____

_____

The best part of my day was

_____

_____

My healthy habit of the day was

_____

_____

The healthy food I chose to nourish my body was

_____

_____

The amount of water I drank was

_____

_____

My active movement of the day was

_____

_____

My overall feeling and mood of the day was

_____

_____

I reduced my stress by

_____

_____

I am going to bed grateful for

_____

_____

Date   /   /

I woke up grateful for

_____

_____

The best part of my day was

_____

_____

My healthy habit of the day was

_____

_____

The healthy food I chose to nourish my body was

_____

_____

The amount of water I drank was

_____

_____

My active movement of the day was

_____

_____

My overall feeling and mood of the day was

_____

_____

I reduced my stress by

_____

_____

I am going to bed grateful for

_____

_____

Date   /   /

I woke up grateful for
_____
_____

The best part of my day was
_____
_____

My healthy habit of the day was
_____
_____

The healthy food I chose to nourish my body was
_____
_____

The amount of water I drank was
_____
_____

My active movement of the day was
_____
_____

My overall feeling and mood of the day was
_____
_____

I reduced my stress by
_____
_____

I am going to bed grateful for
_____
_____

Date   /   /

I woke up grateful for

_____

_____

The best part of my day was

_____

_____

My healthy habit of the day was

_____

_____

The healthy food I chose to nourish my body was

_____

_____

The amount of water I drank was

_____

_____

My active movement of the day was

_____

_____

My overall feeling and mood of the day was

_____

_____

I reduced my stress by

_____

_____

I am going to bed grateful for

_____

_____

Date   /   /

I woke up grateful for

_____

_____

The best part of my day was

_____

_____

My healthy habit of the day was

_____

_____

The healthy food I chose to nourish my body was

_____

_____

The amount of water I drank was

_____

_____

My active movement of the day was

_____

_____

My overall feeling and mood of the day was

_____

_____

I reduced my stress by

_____

_____

I am going to bed grateful for

_____

_____

Date   /   /

I woke up grateful for
_____
_____

The best part of my day was
_____
_____

My healthy habit of the day was
_____
_____

The healthy food I chose to nourish my body was
_____
_____

The amount of water I drank was
_____
_____

My active movement of the day was
_____
_____

My overall feeling and mood of the day was
_____
_____

I reduced my stress by
_____
_____

I am going to bed grateful for
_____
_____

Date / /

I woke up grateful for

_____

_____

The best part of my day was

_____

_____

My healthy habit of the day was

_____

_____

The healthy food I chose to nourish my body was

_____

_____

The amount of water I drank was

_____

_____

My active movement of the day was

_____

_____

My overall feeling and mood of the day was

_____

_____

I reduced my stress by

_____

_____

I am going to bed grateful for

_____

_____

Date   /   /

I woke up grateful for
_____
_____

The best part of my day was
_____
_____

My healthy habit of the day was
_____
_____

The healthy food I chose to nourish my body was
_____
_____

The amount of water I drank was
_____
_____

My active movement of the day was
_____
_____

My overall feeling and mood of the day was
_____
_____

I reduced my stress by
_____
_____

I am going to bed grateful for
_____
_____

Date   /   /

I woke up grateful for

_____

_____

The best part of my day was

_____

_____

My healthy habit of the day was

_____

_____

The healthy food I chose to nourish my body was

_____

_____

The amount of water I drank was

_____

_____

My active movement of the day was

_____

_____

My overall feeling and mood of the day was

_____

_____

I reduced my stress by

_____

_____

I am going to bed grateful for

_____

_____

Date / /

I woke up grateful for
_____
_____

The best part of my day was
_____
_____

My healthy habit of the day was
_____
_____

The healthy food I chose to nourish my body was
_____
_____

The amount of water I drank was
_____
_____

My active movement of the day was
_____
_____

My overall feeling and mood of the day was
_____
_____

I reduced my stress by
_____
_____

I am going to bed grateful for
_____
_____

Date   /   /

I woke up grateful for

_____

_____

The best part of my day was

_____

_____

My healthy habit of the day was

_____

_____

The healthy food I chose to nourish my body was

_____

_____

The amount of water I drank was

_____

_____

My active movement of the day was

_____

_____

My overall feeling and mood of the day was

_____

_____

I reduced my stress by

_____

_____

I am going to bed grateful for

_____

_____

Date   /   /

I woke up grateful for
_____
_____

The best part of my day was
_____
_____

My healthy habit of the day was
_____
_____

The healthy food I chose to nourish my body was
_____
_____

The amount of water I drank was
_____
_____

My active movement of the day was
_____
_____

My overall feeling and mood of the day was
_____
_____

I reduced my stress by
_____
_____

I am going to bed grateful for
_____
_____

Date   /   /

I woke up grateful for

_____

_____

The best part of my day was

_____

_____

My healthy habit of the day was

_____

_____

The healthy food I chose to nourish my body was

_____

_____

The amount of water I drank was

_____

_____

My active movement of the day was

_____

_____

My overall feeling and mood of the day was

_____

_____

I reduced my stress by

_____

_____

I am going to bed grateful for

_____

_____

Date   /   /

I woke up grateful for
_____
_____

The best part of my day was
_____
_____

My healthy habit of the day was
_____
_____

The healthy food I chose to nourish my body was
_____
_____

The amount of water I drank was
_____
_____

My active movement of the day was
_____
_____

My overall feeling and mood of the day was
_____
_____

I reduced my stress by
_____
_____

I am going to bed grateful for
_____
_____

Date / /

I woke up grateful for
_____
_____

The best part of my day was
_____
_____

My healthy habit of the day was
_____
_____

The healthy food I chose to nourish my body was
_____
_____

The amount of water I drank was
_____
_____

My active movement of the day was
_____
_____

My overall feeling and mood of the day was
_____
_____

I reduced my stress by
_____
_____

I am going to bed grateful for
_____
_____

Date   /   /

I woke up grateful for
_____
_____

The best part of my day was
_____
_____

My healthy habit of the day was
_____
_____

The healthy food I chose to nourish my body was
_____
_____

The amount of water I drank was
_____
_____

My active movement of the day was
_____
_____

My overall feeling and mood of the day was
_____
_____

I reduced my stress by
_____
_____

I am going to bed grateful for
_____
_____

Date   /   /

I woke up grateful for

_____

_____

The best part of my day was

_____

_____

My healthy habit of the day was

_____

_____

The healthy food I chose to nourish my body was

_____

_____

The amount of water I drank was

_____

_____

My active movement of the day was

_____

_____

My overall feeling and mood of the day was

_____

_____

I reduced my stress by

_____

_____

I am going to bed grateful for

_____

_____

Date   /   /

I woke up grateful for
_____
_____

The best part of my day was
_____
_____

My healthy habit of the day was
_____
_____

The healthy food I chose to nourish my body was
_____
_____

The amount of water I drank was
_____
_____

My active movement of the day was
_____
_____

My overall feeling and mood of the day was
_____
_____

I reduced my stress by
_____
_____

I am going to bed grateful for
_____
_____

Date   /   /

I woke up grateful for

_____

_____

The best part of my day was

_____

_____

My healthy habit of the day was

_____

_____

The healthy food I chose to nourish my body was

_____

_____

The amount of water I drank was

_____

_____

My active movement of the day was

_____

_____

My overall feeling and mood of the day was

_____

_____

I reduced my stress by

_____

_____

I am going to bed grateful for

_____

_____

Date / /

I woke up grateful for

_____

_____

The best part of my day was

_____

_____

My healthy habit of the day was

_____

_____

The healthy food I chose to nourish my body was

_____

_____

The amount of water I drank was

_____

_____

My active movement of the day was

_____

_____

My overall feeling and mood of the day was

_____

_____

I reduced my stress by

_____

_____

I am going to bed grateful for

_____

_____

Date   /   /

I woke up grateful for

_____

_____

The best part of my day was

_____

_____

My healthy habit of the day was

_____

_____

The healthy food I chose to nourish my body was

_____

_____

The amount of water I drank was

_____

_____

My active movement of the day was

_____

_____

My overall feeling and mood of the day was

_____

_____

I reduced my stress by

_____

_____

I am going to bed grateful for

_____

_____

Date   /   /

I woke up grateful for

_____

_____

The best part of my day was

_____

_____

My healthy habit of the day was

_____

_____

The healthy food I chose to nourish my body was

_____

_____

The amount of water I drank was

_____

_____

My active movement of the day was

_____

_____

My overall feeling and mood of the day was

_____

_____

I reduced my stress by

_____

_____

I am going to bed grateful for

_____

_____

Date   /   /

I woke up grateful for

_____

_____

The best part of my day was

_____

_____

My healthy habit of the day was

_____

_____

The healthy food I chose to nourish my body was

_____

_____

The amount of water I drank was

_____

_____

My active movement of the day was

_____

_____

My overall feeling and mood of the day was

_____

_____

I reduced my stress by

_____

_____

I am going to bed grateful for

_____

_____

Date   /   /

I woke up grateful for

_____

_____

The best part of my day was

_____

_____

My healthy habit of the day was

_____

_____

The healthy food I chose to nourish my body was

_____

_____

The amount of water I drank was

_____

_____

My active movement of the day was

_____

_____

My overall feeling and mood of the day was

_____

_____

I reduced my stress by

_____

_____

I am going to bed grateful for

_____

_____

Date   /   /

I woke up grateful for

_____

_____

The best part of my day was

_____

_____

My healthy habit of the day was

_____

_____

The healthy food I chose to nourish my body was

_____

_____

The amount of water I drank was

_____

_____

My active movement of the day was

_____

_____

My overall feeling and mood of the day was

_____

_____

I reduced my stress by

_____

_____

I am going to bed grateful for

_____

_____

Date   /   /

I woke up grateful for

_____

_____

The best part of my day was

_____

_____

My healthy habit of the day was

_____

_____

The healthy food I chose to nourish my body was

_____

_____

The amount of water I drank was

_____

_____

My active movement of the day was

_____

_____

My overall feeling and mood of the day was

_____

_____

I reduced my stress by

_____

_____

I am going to bed grateful for

_____

_____

Date   /   /

I woke up grateful for

_____

_____

The best part of my day was

_____

_____

My healthy habit of the day was

_____

_____

The healthy food I chose to nourish my body was

_____

_____

The amount of water I drank was

_____

_____

My active movement of the day was

_____

_____

My overall feeling and mood of the day was

_____

_____

I reduced my stress by

_____

_____

I am going to bed grateful for

_____

_____

Date / /

I woke up grateful for

_____

_____

The best part of my day was

_____

_____

My healthy habit of the day was

_____

_____

The healthy food I chose to nourish my body was

_____

_____

The amount of water I drank was

_____

_____

My active movement of the day was

_____

_____

My overall feeling and mood of the day was

_____

_____

I reduced my stress by

_____

_____

I am going to bed grateful for

_____

_____

Date   /   /

I woke up grateful for

_____

_____

The best part of my day was

_____

_____

My healthy habit of the day was

_____

_____

The healthy food I chose to nourish my body was

_____

_____

The amount of water I drank was

_____

_____

My active movement of the day was

_____

_____

My overall feeling and mood of the day was

_____

_____

I reduced my stress by

_____

_____

I am going to bed grateful for

_____

_____

Date   /   /

I woke up grateful for

_____

_____

The best part of my day was

_____

_____

My healthy habit of the day was

_____

_____

The healthy food I chose to nourish my body was

_____

_____

The amount of water I drank was

_____

_____

My active movement of the day was

_____

_____

My overall feeling and mood of the day was

_____

_____

I reduced my stress by

_____

_____

I am going to bed grateful for

_____

_____

Date   /   /

I woke up grateful for

_____

_____

The best part of my day was

_____

_____

My healthy habit of the day was

_____

_____

The healthy food I chose to nourish my body was

_____

_____

The amount of water I drank was

_____

_____

My active movement of the day was

_____

_____

My overall feeling and mood of the day was

_____

_____

I reduced my stress by

_____

_____

I am going to bed grateful for

_____

_____

Date   /   /

I woke up grateful for
_____
_____

The best part of my day was
_____
_____

My healthy habit of the day was
_____
_____

The healthy food I chose to nourish my body was
_____
_____

The amount of water I drank was
_____
_____

My active movement of the day was
_____
_____

My overall feeling and mood of the day was
_____
_____

I reduced my stress by
_____
_____

I am going to bed grateful for
_____
_____

Date   /   /

I woke up grateful for
_____
_____

The best part of my day was
_____
_____

My healthy habit of the day was
_____
_____

The healthy food I chose to nourish my body was
_____
_____

The amount of water I drank was
_____
_____

My active movement of the day was
_____
_____

My overall feeling and mood of the day was
_____
_____

I reduced my stress by
_____
_____

I am going to bed grateful for
_____
_____

Date   /   /

I woke up grateful for
_____
_____

The best part of my day was
_____
_____

My healthy habit of the day was
_____
_____

The healthy food I chose to nourish my body was
_____
_____

The amount of water I drank was
_____
_____

My active movement of the day was
_____
_____

My overall feeling and mood of the day was
_____
_____

I reduced my stress by
_____
_____

I am going to bed grateful for
_____
_____

Date / /

I woke up grateful for

_____

_____

The best part of my day was

_____

_____

My healthy habit of the day was

_____

_____

The healthy food I chose to nourish my body was

_____

_____

The amount of water I drank was

_____

_____

My active movement of the day was

_____

_____

My overall feeling and mood of the day was

_____

_____

I reduced my stress by

_____

_____

I am going to bed grateful for

_____

_____

Date   /   /

I woke up grateful for

_____

_____

The best part of my day was

_____

_____

My healthy habit of the day was

_____

_____

The healthy food I chose to nourish my body was

_____

_____

The amount of water I drank was

_____

_____

My active movement of the day was

_____

_____

My overall feeling and mood of the day was

_____

_____

I reduced my stress by

_____

_____

I am going to bed grateful for

_____

_____

Date   /   /

I woke up grateful for

_____

_____

The best part of my day was

_____

_____

My healthy habit of the day was

_____

_____

The healthy food I chose to nourish my body was

_____

_____

The amount of water I drank was

_____

_____

My active movement of the day was

_____

_____

My overall feeling and mood of the day was

_____

_____

I reduced my stress by

_____

_____

I am going to bed grateful for

_____

_____

Date   /   /

I woke up grateful for

_____

_____

The best part of my day was

_____

_____

My healthy habit of the day was

_____

_____

The healthy food I chose to nourish my body was

_____

_____

The amount of water I drank was

_____

_____

My active movement of the day was

_____

_____

My overall feeling and mood of the day was

_____

_____

I reduced my stress by

_____

_____

I am going to bed grateful for

_____

_____

Date / /

I woke up grateful for

_____

_____

The best part of my day was

_____

_____

My healthy habit of the day was

_____

_____

The healthy food I chose to nourish my body was

_____

_____

The amount of water I drank was

_____

_____

My active movement of the day was

_____

_____

My overall feeling and mood of the day was

_____

_____

I reduced my stress by

_____

_____

I am going to bed grateful for

_____

_____

Date   / /

I woke up grateful for

_____

_____

The best part of my day was

_____

_____

My healthy habit of the day was

_____

_____

The healthy food I chose to nourish my body was

_____

_____

The amount of water I drank was

_____

_____

My active movement of the day was

_____

_____

My overall feeling and mood of the day was

_____

_____

I reduced my stress by

_____

_____

I am going to bed grateful for

_____

_____

Date   /   /

I woke up grateful for

_____

_____

The best part of my day was

_____

_____

My healthy habit of the day was

_____

_____

The healthy food I chose to nourish my body was

_____

_____

The amount of water I drank was

_____

_____

My active movement of the day was

_____

_____

My overall feeling and mood of the day was

_____

_____

I reduced my stress by

_____

_____

I am going to bed grateful for

_____

_____

Date   /   /

I woke up grateful for
_____
_____

The best part of my day was
_____
_____

My healthy habit of the day was
_____
_____

The healthy food I chose to nourish my body was
_____
_____

The amount of water I drank was
_____
_____

My active movement of the day was
_____
_____

My overall feeling and mood of the day was
_____
_____

I reduced my stress by
_____
_____

I am going to bed grateful for
_____
_____

Date   /   /

I woke up grateful for

_____

_____

The best part of my day was

_____

_____

My healthy habit of the day was

_____

_____

The healthy food I chose to nourish my body was

_____

_____

The amount of water I drank was

_____

_____

My active movement of the day was

_____

_____

My overall feeling and mood of the day was

_____

_____

I reduced my stress by

_____

_____

I am going to bed grateful for

_____

_____

Date   /   /

I woke up grateful for
_____
_____

The best part of my day was
_____
_____

My healthy habit of the day was
_____
_____

The healthy food I chose to nourish my body was
_____
_____

The amount of water I drank was
_____
_____

My active movement of the day was
_____
_____

My overall feeling and mood of the day was
_____
_____

I reduced my stress by
_____
_____

I am going to bed grateful for
_____
_____

Date   /   /

I woke up grateful for

_____

_____

The best part of my day was

_____

My healthy habit of the day was

_____

The healthy food I chose to nourish my body was

_____

The amount of water I drank was

_____

My active movement of the day was

_____

My overall feeling and mood of the day was

_____

I reduced my stress by

_____

I am going to bed grateful for

_____

_____

Date   /   /

I woke up grateful for

_____

_____

The best part of my day was

_____

_____

My healthy habit of the day was

_____

_____

The healthy food I chose to nourish my body was

_____

_____

The amount of water I drank was

_____

_____

My active movement of the day was

_____

_____

My overall feeling and mood of the day was

_____

_____

I reduced my stress by

_____

_____

I am going to bed grateful for

_____

_____

Date   /   /

I woke up grateful for

_____

_____

The best part of my day was

_____

_____

My healthy habit of the day was

_____

_____

The healthy food I chose to nourish my body was

_____

_____

The amount of water I drank was

_____

_____

My active movement of the day was

_____

_____

My overall feeling and mood of the day was

_____

_____

I reduced my stress by

_____

_____

I am going to bed grateful for

_____

_____

Date   /   /

I woke up grateful for

_____

The best part of my day was

_____

My healthy habit of the day was

_____

The healthy food I chose to nourish my body was

_____

The amount of water I drank was

_____

My active movement of the day was

_____

My overall feeling and mood of the day was

_____

I reduced my stress by

_____

I am going to bed grateful for

_____

Date   /   /

I woke up grateful for

_____

_____

The best part of my day was

_____

_____

My healthy habit of the day was

_____

_____

The healthy food I chose to nourish my body was

_____

_____

The amount of water I drank was

_____

_____

My active movement of the day was

_____

_____

My overall feeling and mood of the day was

_____

_____

I reduced my stress by

_____

_____

I am going to bed grateful for

_____

_____

Date   /   /

I woke up grateful for

_____

_____

The best part of my day was

_____

_____

My healthy habit of the day was

_____

_____

The healthy food I chose to nourish my body was

_____

_____

The amount of water I drank was

_____

_____

My active movement of the day was

_____

_____

My overall feeling and mood of the day was

_____

_____

I reduced my stress by

_____

_____

I am going to bed grateful for

_____

_____

Date   /   /

I woke up grateful for

_____

_____

The best part of my day was

_____

_____

My healthy habit of the day was

_____

_____

The healthy food I chose to nourish my body was

_____

_____

The amount of water I drank was

_____

_____

My active movement of the day was

_____

_____

My overall feeling and mood of the day was

_____

_____

I reduced my stress by

_____

_____

I am going to bed grateful for

_____

_____

Date   /   /

I woke up grateful for

_____

_____

The best part of my day was

_____

_____

My healthy habit of the day was

_____

_____

The healthy food I chose to nourish my body was

_____

_____

The amount of water I drank was

_____

_____

My active movement of the day was

_____

_____

My overall feeling and mood of the day was

_____

_____

I reduced my stress by

_____

_____

I am going to bed grateful for

_____

_____

Date   /   /

I woke up grateful for

_____

_____

The best part of my day was

_____

_____

My healthy habit of the day was

_____

_____

The healthy food I chose to nourish my body was

_____

_____

The amount of water I drank was

_____

_____

My active movement of the day was

_____

_____

My overall feeling and mood of the day was

_____

_____

I reduced my stress by

_____

_____

I am going to bed grateful for

_____

_____

Date   /   /

I woke up grateful for
_____

_____

The best part of my day was
_____

_____

My healthy habit of the day was
_____

_____

The healthy food I chose to nourish my body was
_____

_____

The amount of water I drank was
_____

_____

My active movement of the day was
_____

_____

My overall feeling and mood of the day was
_____

_____

I reduced my stress by
_____

_____

I am going to bed grateful for
_____

_____

Date   /   /

I woke up grateful for

_____

_____

The best part of my day was

_____

_____

My healthy habit of the day was

_____

_____

The healthy food I chose to nourish my body was

_____

_____

The amount of water I drank was

_____

_____

My active movement of the day was

_____

_____

My overall feeling and mood of the day was

_____

_____

I reduced my stress by

_____

_____

I am going to bed grateful for

_____

_____

Date   /   /

I woke up grateful for
_____
_____

The best part of my day was
_____
_____

My healthy habit of the day was
_____
_____

The healthy food I chose to nourish my body was
_____
_____

The amount of water I drank was
_____
_____

My active movement of the day was
_____
_____

My overall feeling and mood of the day was
_____
_____

I reduced my stress by
_____
_____

I am going to bed grateful for
_____
_____

Date   /   /

I woke up grateful for
_____
_____

The best part of my day was
_____
_____

My healthy habit of the day was
_____
_____

The healthy food I chose to nourish my body was
_____
_____

The amount of water I drank was
_____
_____

My active movement of the day was
_____
_____

My overall feeling and mood of the day was
_____
_____

I reduced my stress by
_____
_____

I am going to bed grateful for
_____
_____

Date / /

I woke up grateful for
_____
_____

The best part of my day was
_____
_____

My healthy habit of the day was
_____
_____

The healthy food I chose to nourish my body was
_____
_____

The amount of water I drank was
_____
_____

My active movement of the day was
_____
_____

My overall feeling and mood of the day was
_____
_____

I reduced my stress by
_____
_____

I am going to bed grateful for
_____
_____

Date   / /

I woke up grateful for

_____

_____

The best part of my day was

_____

_____

My healthy habit of the day was

_____

_____

The healthy food I chose to nourish my body was

_____

_____

The amount of water I drank was

_____

_____

My active movement of the day was

_____

_____

My overall feeling and mood of the day was

_____

_____

I reduced my stress by

_____

_____

I am going to bed grateful for

_____

_____

Date   /   /

I woke up grateful for
_____
_____

The best part of my day was
_____
_____

My healthy habit of the day was
_____
_____

The healthy food I chose to nourish my body was
_____
_____

The amount of water I drank was
_____
_____

My active movement of the day was
_____
_____

My overall feeling and mood of the day was
_____
_____

I reduced my stress by
_____
_____

I am going to bed grateful for
_____
_____

Date / /

I woke up grateful for

_____

_____

The best part of my day was

_____

_____

My healthy habit of the day was

_____

_____

The healthy food I chose to nourish my body was

_____

_____

The amount of water I drank was

_____

_____

My active movement of the day was

_____

_____

My overall feeling and mood of the day was

_____

_____

I reduced my stress by

_____

_____

I am going to bed grateful for

_____

_____

Date   /   /

I woke up grateful for

_____

_____

The best part of my day was

_____

_____

My healthy habit of the day was

_____

_____

The healthy food I chose to nourish my body was

_____

_____

The amount of water I drank was

_____

_____

My active movement of the day was

_____

_____

My overall feeling and mood of the day was

_____

_____

I reduced my stress by

_____

_____

I am going to bed grateful for

_____

_____

Date   /   /

I woke up grateful for

_____

_____

The best part of my day was

_____

_____

My healthy habit of the day was

_____

_____

The healthy food I chose to nourish my body was

_____

_____

The amount of water I drank was

_____

_____

My active movement of the day was

_____

_____

My overall feeling and mood of the day was

_____

_____

I reduced my stress by

_____

_____

I am going to bed grateful for

_____

_____

Date / /

I woke up grateful for

_____

_____

The best part of my day was

_____

_____

My healthy habit of the day was

_____

_____

The healthy food I chose to nourish my body was

_____

_____

The amount of water I drank was

_____

_____

My active movement of the day was

_____

_____

My overall feeling and mood of the day was

_____

_____

I reduced my stress by

_____

_____

I am going to bed grateful for

_____

_____

Date / /

I woke up grateful for
_____
_____

The best part of my day was
_____
_____

My healthy habit of the day was
_____
_____

The healthy food I chose to nourish my body was
_____
_____

The amount of water I drank was
_____
_____

My active movement of the day was
_____
_____

My overall feeling and mood of the day was
_____
_____

I reduced my stress by
_____
_____

I am going to bed grateful for
_____
_____

Date / /

I woke up grateful for

_____

_____

The best part of my day was

_____

_____

My healthy habit of the day was

_____

_____

The healthy food I chose to nourish my body was

_____

_____

The amount of water I drank was

_____

_____

My active movement of the day was

_____

_____

My overall feeling and mood of the day was

_____

_____

I reduced my stress by

_____

_____

I am going to bed grateful for

_____

_____

Date   /   /

I woke up grateful for

_____

_____

The best part of my day was

_____

_____

My healthy habit of the day was

_____

_____

The healthy food I chose to nourish my body was

_____

_____

The amount of water I drank was

_____

_____

My active movement of the day was

_____

_____

My overall feeling and mood of the day was

_____

_____

I reduced my stress by

_____

_____

I am going to bed grateful for

_____

_____

Date   /   /

I woke up grateful for

_____

_____

The best part of my day was

_____

_____

My healthy habit of the day was

_____

_____

The healthy food I chose to nourish my body was

_____

_____

The amount of water I drank was

_____

_____

My active movement of the day was

_____

_____

My overall feeling and mood of the day was

_____

_____

I reduced my stress by

_____

_____

I am going to bed grateful for

_____

_____

Date   /   /

I woke up grateful for

_____

_____

The best part of my day was

_____

_____

My healthy habit of the day was

_____

_____

The healthy food I chose to nourish my body was

_____

_____

The amount of water I drank was

_____

_____

My active movement of the day was

_____

_____

My overall feeling and mood of the day was

_____

_____

I reduced my stress by

_____

_____

I am going to bed grateful for

_____

_____

Date   /   /

I woke up grateful for
_____
_____

The best part of my day was
_____
_____

My healthy habit of the day was
_____
_____

The healthy food I chose to nourish my body was
_____
_____

The amount of water I drank was
_____
_____

My active movement of the day was
_____
_____

My overall feeling and mood of the day was
_____
_____

I reduced my stress by
_____
_____

I am going to bed grateful for
_____
_____

Date / /

I woke up grateful for

_____

_____

The best part of my day was

_____

_____

My healthy habit of the day was

_____

_____

The healthy food I chose to nourish my body was

_____

_____

The amount of water I drank was

_____

_____

My active movement of the day was

_____

_____

My overall feeling and mood of the day was

_____

_____

I reduced my stress by

_____

_____

I am going to bed grateful for

_____

_____

Date   /   /

I woke up grateful for

_____

_____

The best part of my day was

_____

_____

My healthy habit of the day was

_____

_____

The healthy food I chose to nourish my body was

_____

_____

The amount of water I drank was

_____

_____

My active movement of the day was

_____

_____

My overall feeling and mood of the day was

_____

_____

I reduced my stress by

_____

_____

I am going to bed grateful for

_____

_____

Date   /   /

I woke up grateful for

_____

_____

The best part of my day was

_____

_____

My healthy habit of the day was

_____

_____

The healthy food I chose to nourish my body was

_____

_____

The amount of water I drank was

_____

_____

My active movement of the day was

_____

_____

My overall feeling and mood of the day was

_____

_____

I reduced my stress by

_____

_____

I am going to bed grateful for

_____

_____

Date   /   /

I woke up grateful for
_____
_____

The best part of my day was
_____
_____

My healthy habit of the day was
_____
_____

The healthy food I chose to nourish my body was
_____
_____

The amount of water I drank was
_____
_____

My active movement of the day was
_____
_____

My overall feeling and mood of the day was
_____
_____

I reduced my stress by
_____
_____

I am going to bed grateful for
_____
_____

Date   /   /

I woke up grateful for
_____
_____

The best part of my day was
_____
_____

My healthy habit of the day was
_____
_____

The healthy food I chose to nourish my body was
_____
_____

The amount of water I drank was
_____
_____

My active movement of the day was
_____
_____

My overall feeling and mood of the day was
_____
_____

I reduced my stress by
_____
_____

I am going to bed grateful for
_____
_____

Date   /   /

I woke up grateful for

_____

_____

The best part of my day was

_____

_____

My healthy habit of the day was

_____

_____

The healthy food I chose to nourish my body was

_____

_____

The amount of water I drank was

_____

_____

My active movement of the day was

_____

_____

My overall feeling and mood of the day was

_____

_____

I reduced my stress by

_____

_____

I am going to bed grateful for

_____

_____

Date   /   /

I woke up grateful for

_____

_____

The best part of my day was

_____

_____

My healthy habit of the day was

_____

_____

The healthy food I chose to nourish my body was

_____

_____

The amount of water I drank was

_____

_____

My active movement of the day was

_____

_____

My overall feeling and mood of the day was

_____

_____

I reduced my stress by

_____

_____

I am going to bed grateful for

_____

_____

Date   /   /

I woke up grateful for

_____

_____

The best part of my day was

_____

_____

My healthy habit of the day was

_____

_____

The healthy food I chose to nourish my body was

_____

_____

The amount of water I drank was

_____

_____

My active movement of the day was

_____

_____

My overall feeling and mood of the day was

_____

_____

I reduced my stress by

_____

_____

I am going to bed grateful for

_____

_____

Date   /   /

I woke up grateful for

_____

_____

The best part of my day was

_____

_____

My healthy habit of the day was

_____

_____

The healthy food I chose to nourish my body was

_____

_____

The amount of water I drank was

_____

_____

My active movement of the day was

_____

_____

My overall feeling and mood of the day was

_____

_____

I reduced my stress by

_____

_____

I am going to bed grateful for

_____

_____

Date   /   /

I woke up grateful for
_____
_____

The best part of my day was
_____
_____

My healthy habit of the day was
_____
_____

The healthy food I chose to nourish my body was
_____
_____

The amount of water I drank was
_____
_____

My active movement of the day was
_____
_____

My overall feeling and mood of the day was
_____
_____

I reduced my stress by
_____
_____

I am going to bed grateful for
_____
_____

Date   /   /

I woke up grateful for

_____

_____

The best part of my day was

_____

_____

My healthy habit of the day was

_____

_____

The healthy food I chose to nourish my body was

_____

_____

The amount of water I drank was

_____

_____

My active movement of the day was

_____

_____

My overall feeling and mood of the day was

_____

_____

I reduced my stress by

_____

_____

I am going to bed grateful for

_____

_____

Date   /   /

I woke up grateful for
_____

_____

The best part of my day was
_____

_____

My healthy habit of the day was
_____

_____

The healthy food I chose to nourish my body was
_____

_____

The amount of water I drank was
_____

_____

My active movement of the day was
_____

_____

My overall feeling and mood of the day was
_____

_____

I reduced my stress by
_____

_____

I am going to bed grateful for
_____

_____

Date / /

I woke up grateful for

_____

_____

The best part of my day was

_____

_____

My healthy habit of the day was

_____

_____

The healthy food I chose to nourish my body was

_____

_____

The amount of water I drank was

_____

_____

My active movement of the day was

_____

_____

My overall feeling and mood of the day was

_____

_____

I reduced my stress by

_____

_____

I am going to bed grateful for

_____

_____

Date   /   /

I woke up grateful for
_____
_____

The best part of my day was
_____
_____

My healthy habit of the day was
_____
_____

The healthy food I chose to nourish my body was
_____
_____

The amount of water I drank was
_____
_____

My active movement of the day was
_____
_____

My overall feeling and mood of the day was
_____
_____

I reduced my stress by
_____
_____

I am going to bed grateful for
_____
_____

Date   /   /

I woke up grateful for

_____

_____

The best part of my day was

_____

_____

My healthy habit of the day was

_____

_____

The healthy food I chose to nourish my body was

_____

_____

The amount of water I drank was

_____

_____

My active movement of the day was

_____

_____

My overall feeling and mood of the day was

_____

_____

I reduced my stress by

_____

_____

I am going to bed grateful for

_____

_____

Date   /   /

I woke up grateful for

_____

_____

The best part of my day was

_____

_____

My healthy habit of the day was

_____

_____

The healthy food I chose to nourish my body was

_____

_____

The amount of water I drank was

_____

_____

My active movement of the day was

_____

_____

My overall feeling and mood of the day was

_____

_____

I reduced my stress by

_____

_____

I am going to bed grateful for

_____

_____

Date   /   /

I woke up grateful for

_____

_____

The best part of my day was

_____

_____

My healthy habit of the day was

_____

_____

The healthy food I chose to nourish my body was

_____

_____

The amount of water I drank was

_____

_____

My active movement of the day was

_____

_____

My overall feeling and mood of the day was

_____

_____

I reduced my stress by

_____

_____

I am going to bed grateful for

_____

_____

Date   /   /

I woke up grateful for

_____

_____

The best part of my day was

_____

_____

My healthy habit of the day was

_____

_____

The healthy food I chose to nourish my body was

_____

_____

The amount of water I drank was

_____

_____

My active movement of the day was

_____

_____

My overall feeling and mood of the day was

_____

_____

I reduced my stress by

_____

_____

I am going to bed grateful for

_____

_____

Date / /

I woke up grateful for

_____

_____

The best part of my day was

_____

_____

My healthy habit of the day was

_____

_____

The healthy food I chose to nourish my body was

_____

_____

The amount of water I drank was

_____

_____

My active movement of the day was

_____

_____

My overall feeling and mood of the day was

_____

_____

I reduced my stress by

_____

_____

I am going to bed grateful for

_____

_____

Date / /

I woke up grateful for

_____

_____

The best part of my day was

_____

_____

My healthy habit of the day was

_____

_____

The healthy food I chose to nourish my body was

_____

_____

The amount of water I drank was

_____

_____

My active movement of the day was

_____

_____

My overall feeling and mood of the day was

_____

_____

I reduced my stress by

_____

_____

I am going to bed grateful for

_____

_____

Date   /   /

I woke up grateful for

_____

_____

The best part of my day was

_____

_____

My healthy habit of the day was

_____

_____

The healthy food I chose to nourish my body was

_____

_____

The amount of water I drank was

_____

_____

My active movement of the day was

_____

_____

My overall feeling and mood of the day was

_____

_____

I reduced my stress by

_____

_____

I am going to bed grateful for

_____

_____

Date   /   /

I woke up grateful for
_____
_____

The best part of my day was
_____
_____

My healthy habit of the day was
_____
_____

The healthy food I chose to nourish my body was
_____
_____

The amount of water I drank was
_____
_____

My active movement of the day was
_____
_____

My overall feeling and mood of the day was
_____
_____

I reduced my stress by
_____
_____

I am going to bed grateful for
_____
_____

Date   /   /

I woke up grateful for
_____
_____

The best part of my day was
_____
_____

My healthy habit of the day was
_____
_____

The healthy food I chose to nourish my body was
_____
_____

The amount of water I drank was
_____
_____

My active movement of the day was
_____
_____

My overall feeling and mood of the day was
_____
_____

I reduced my stress by
_____
_____

I am going to bed grateful for
_____
_____

Date   /   /

I woke up grateful for

_____

_____

The best part of my day was

_____

_____

My healthy habit of the day was

_____

_____

The healthy food I chose to nourish my body was

_____

_____

The amount of water I drank was

_____

_____

My active movement of the day was

_____

_____

My overall feeling and mood of the day was

_____

_____

I reduced my stress by

_____

_____

I am going to bed grateful for

_____

_____

Date   /   /

I woke up grateful for

_____

_____

The best part of my day was

_____

_____

My healthy habit of the day was

_____

_____

The healthy food I chose to nourish my body was

_____

_____

The amount of water I drank was

_____

_____

My active movement of the day was

_____

_____

My overall feeling and mood of the day was

_____

_____

I reduced my stress by

_____

_____

I am going to bed grateful for

_____

_____

Date   /   /

I woke up grateful for

_____

_____

The best part of my day was

_____

_____

My healthy habit of the day was

_____

_____

The healthy food I chose to nourish my body was

_____

_____

The amount of water I drank was

_____

_____

My active movement of the day was

_____

_____

My overall feeling and mood of the day was

_____

_____

I reduced my stress by

_____

_____

I am going to bed grateful for

_____

_____

Date   /   /

I woke up grateful for
_____

_____

The best part of my day was
_____

_____

My healthy habit of the day was
_____

_____

The healthy food I chose to nourish my body was
_____

_____

The amount of water I drank was
_____

_____

My active movement of the day was
_____

_____

My overall feeling and mood of the day was
_____

_____

I reduced my stress by
_____

_____

I am going to bed grateful for
_____

_____

Date   /   /

I woke up grateful for

_____

_____

The best part of my day was

_____

_____

My healthy habit of the day was

_____

_____

The healthy food I chose to nourish my body was

_____

_____

The amount of water I drank was

_____

_____

My active movement of the day was

_____

_____

My overall feeling and mood of the day was

_____

_____

I reduced my stress by

_____

_____

I am going to bed grateful for

_____

_____

Date / /

I woke up grateful for

_____

_____

The best part of my day was

_____

_____

My healthy habit of the day was

_____

_____

The healthy food I chose to nourish my body was

_____

_____

The amount of water I drank was

_____

_____

My active movement of the day was

_____

_____

My overall feeling and mood of the day was

_____

_____

I reduced my stress by

_____

_____

I am going to bed grateful for

_____

_____

Date / /

I woke up grateful for

_____

_____

The best part of my day was

_____

_____

My healthy habit of the day was

_____

_____

The healthy food I chose to nourish my body was

_____

_____

The amount of water I drank was

_____

_____

My active movement of the day was

_____

_____

My overall feeling and mood of the day was

_____

_____

I reduced my stress by

_____

_____

I am going to bed grateful for

_____

_____

Date / /

I woke up grateful for

_____

_____

The best part of my day was

_____

_____

My healthy habit of the day was

_____

_____

The healthy food I chose to nourish my body was

_____

_____

The amount of water I drank was

_____

_____

My active movement of the day was

_____

_____

My overall feeling and mood of the day was

_____

_____

I reduced my stress by

_____

_____

I am going to bed grateful for

_____

_____

Date   /   /

I woke up grateful for

_____

_____

The best part of my day was

_____

_____

My healthy habit of the day was

_____

_____

The healthy food I chose to nourish my body was

_____

_____

The amount of water I drank was

_____

_____

My active movement of the day was

_____

_____

My overall feeling and mood of the day was

_____

_____

I reduced my stress by

_____

_____

I am going to bed grateful for

_____

_____

Date / /

I woke up grateful for

_____

_____

The best part of my day was

_____

_____

My healthy habit of the day was

_____

_____

The healthy food I chose to nourish my body was

_____

_____

The amount of water I drank was

_____

_____

My active movement of the day was

_____

_____

My overall feeling and mood of the day was

_____

_____

I reduced my stress by

_____

_____

I am going to bed grateful for

_____

_____

Date   /   /

I woke up grateful for
_____
_____

The best part of my day was
_____
_____

My healthy habit of the day was
_____
_____

The healthy food I chose to nourish my body was
_____
_____

The amount of water I drank was
_____
_____

My active movement of the day was
_____
_____

My overall feeling and mood of the day was
_____
_____

I reduced my stress by
_____
_____

I am going to bed grateful for
_____
_____

Date   /   /

I woke up grateful for
_____
_____

The best part of my day was
_____
_____

My healthy habit of the day was
_____
_____

The healthy food I chose to nourish my body was
_____
_____

The amount of water I drank was
_____
_____

My active movement of the day was
_____
_____

My overall feeling and mood of the day was
_____
_____

I reduced my stress by
_____
_____

I am going to bed grateful for
_____
_____

Date / /

I woke up grateful for
_____
_____

The best part of my day was
_____
_____

My healthy habit of the day was
_____
_____

The healthy food I chose to nourish my body was
_____
_____

The amount of water I drank was
_____
_____

My active movement of the day was
_____
_____

My overall feeling and mood of the day was
_____
_____

I reduced my stress by
_____
_____

I am going to bed grateful for
_____
_____

Date   /   /

I woke up grateful for

_____

_____

The best part of my day was

_____

_____

My healthy habit of the day was

_____

_____

The healthy food I chose to nourish my body was

_____

_____

The amount of water I drank was

_____

_____

My active movement of the day was

_____

_____

My overall feeling and mood of the day was

_____

_____

I reduced my stress by

_____

_____

I am going to bed grateful for

_____

_____

Date   /   /

I woke up grateful for
_____
_____

The best part of my day was
_____
_____

My healthy habit of the day was
_____
_____

The healthy food I chose to nourish my body was
_____
_____

The amount of water I drank was
_____
_____

My active movement of the day was
_____
_____

My overall feeling and mood of the day was
_____
_____

I reduced my stress by
_____
_____

I am going to bed grateful for
_____
_____

Date   /   /

I woke up grateful for

_____

_____

The best part of my day was

_____

_____

My healthy habit of the day was

_____

_____

The healthy food I chose to nourish my body was

_____

_____

The amount of water I drank was

_____

_____

My active movement of the day was

_____

_____

My overall feeling and mood of the day was

_____

_____

I reduced my stress by

_____

_____

I am going to bed grateful for

_____

_____

Date / /

I woke up grateful for

_____

_____

The best part of my day was

_____

_____

My healthy habit of the day was

_____

_____

The healthy food I chose to nourish my body was

_____

_____

The amount of water I drank was

_____

_____

My active movement of the day was

_____

_____

My overall feeling and mood of the day was

_____

_____

I reduced my stress by

_____

_____

I am going to bed grateful for

_____

_____

Date /   /

I woke up grateful for

_____

_____

The best part of my day was

_____

_____

My healthy habit of the day was

_____

_____

The healthy food I chose to nourish my body was

_____

_____

The amount of water I drank was

_____

_____

My active movement of the day was

_____

_____

My overall feeling and mood of the day was

_____

_____

I reduced my stress by

_____

_____

I am going to bed grateful for

_____

_____

Date   /   /

I woke up grateful for

_____

_____

The best part of my day was

_____

_____

My healthy habit of the day was

_____

_____

The healthy food I chose to nourish my body was

_____

_____

The amount of water I drank was

_____

_____

My active movement of the day was

_____

_____

My overall feeling and mood of the day was

_____

_____

I reduced my stress by

_____

_____

I am going to bed grateful for

_____

_____

Date   /   /

I woke up grateful for

_____

_____

The best part of my day was

_____

_____

My healthy habit of the day was

_____

_____

The healthy food I chose to nourish my body was

_____

_____

The amount of water I drank was

_____

_____

My active movement of the day was

_____

_____

My overall feeling and mood of the day was

_____

_____

I reduced my stress by

_____

_____

I am going to bed grateful for

_____

_____

Date / /

I woke up grateful for
_____

The best part of my day was
_____

My healthy habit of the day was
_____

The healthy food I chose to nourish my body was
_____

The amount of water I drank was
_____

My active movement of the day was
_____

My overall feeling and mood of the day was
_____

I reduced my stress by
_____

I am going to bed grateful for
_____

Date   /   /

I woke up grateful for
_____
_____

The best part of my day was
_____
_____

My healthy habit of the day was
_____
_____

The healthy food I chose to nourish my body was
_____
_____

The amount of water I drank was
_____
_____

My active movement of the day was
_____
_____

My overall feeling and mood of the day was
_____
_____

I reduced my stress by
_____
_____

I am going to bed grateful for
_____
_____

Date   /   /

I woke up grateful for

_____

_____

The best part of my day was

_____

_____

My healthy habit of the day was

_____

_____

The healthy food I chose to nourish my body was

_____

_____

The amount of water I drank was

_____

_____

My active movement of the day was

_____

_____

My overall feeling and mood of the day was

_____

_____

I reduced my stress by

_____

_____

I am going to bed grateful for

_____

_____

Date   /   /

I woke up grateful for

_____

_____

The best part of my day was

_____

_____

My healthy habit of the day was

_____

_____

The healthy food I chose to nourish my body was

_____

_____

The amount of water I drank was

_____

_____

My active movement of the day was

_____

_____

My overall feeling and mood of the day was

_____

_____

I reduced my stress by

_____

_____

I am going to bed grateful for

_____

_____

Date / /

I woke up grateful for
_____
_____

The best part of my day was
_____
_____

My healthy habit of the day was
_____
_____

The healthy food I chose to nourish my body was
_____
_____

The amount of water I drank was
_____
_____

My active movement of the day was
_____
_____

My overall feeling and mood of the day was
_____
_____

I reduced my stress by
_____
_____

I am going to bed grateful for
_____
_____

Date   /   /

I woke up grateful for

_____

_____

The best part of my day was

_____

_____

My healthy habit of the day was

_____

_____

The healthy food I chose to nourish my body was

_____

_____

The amount of water I drank was

_____

_____

My active movement of the day was

_____

_____

My overall feeling and mood of the day was

_____

_____

I reduced my stress by

_____

_____

I am going to bed grateful for

_____

_____

Date   /   /

I woke up grateful for

_____

_____

The best part of my day was

_____

_____

My healthy habit of the day was

_____

_____

The healthy food I chose to nourish my body was

_____

_____

The amount of water I drank was

_____

_____

My active movement of the day was

_____

_____

My overall feeling and mood of the day was

_____

_____

I reduced my stress by

_____

_____

I am going to bed grateful for

_____

_____

Date / /

I woke up grateful for

_____

_____

The best part of my day was

_____

_____

My healthy habit of the day was

_____

_____

The healthy food I chose to nourish my body was

_____

_____

The amount of water I drank was

_____

_____

My active movement of the day was

_____

_____

My overall feeling and mood of the day was

_____

_____

I reduced my stress by

_____

_____

I am going to bed grateful for

_____

_____

Date / /

I woke up grateful for
_____
_____

The best part of my day was
_____
_____

My healthy habit of the day was
_____
_____

The healthy food I chose to nourish my body was
_____
_____

The amount of water I drank was
_____
_____

My active movement of the day was
_____
_____

My overall feeling and mood of the day was
_____
_____

I reduced my stress by
_____
_____

I am going to bed grateful for
_____
_____

Date / /

I woke up grateful for

_____

_____

The best part of my day was

_____

_____

My healthy habit of the day was

_____

_____

The healthy food I chose to nourish my body was

_____

_____

The amount of water I drank was

_____

_____

My active movement of the day was

_____

_____

My overall feeling and mood of the day was

_____

_____

I reduced my stress by

_____

_____

I am going to bed grateful for

_____

_____

Date   /   /

I woke up grateful for

_____

_____

The best part of my day was

_____

_____

My healthy habit of the day was

_____

_____

The healthy food I chose to nourish my body was

_____

_____

The amount of water I drank was

_____

_____

My active movement of the day was

_____

_____

My overall feeling and mood of the day was

_____

_____

I reduced my stress by

_____

_____

I am going to bed grateful for

_____

_____

Date / /

I woke up grateful for
_____
_____

The best part of my day was
_____
_____

My healthy habit of the day was
_____
_____

The healthy food I chose to nourish my body was
_____
_____

The amount of water I drank was
_____
_____

My active movement of the day was
_____
_____

My overall feeling and mood of the day was
_____
_____

I reduced my stress by
_____
_____

I am going to bed grateful for
_____
_____

Date   /   /

I woke up grateful for

_____

_____

The best part of my day was

_____

_____

My healthy habit of the day was

_____

_____

The healthy food I chose to nourish my body was

_____

_____

The amount of water I drank was

_____

_____

My active movement of the day was

_____

_____

My overall feeling and mood of the day was

_____

_____

I reduced my stress by

_____

_____

I am going to bed grateful for

_____

_____

Date   /   /

I woke up grateful for

_____

_____

The best part of my day was

_____

_____

My healthy habit of the day was

_____

_____

The healthy food I chose to nourish my body was

_____

_____

The amount of water I drank was

_____

_____

My active movement of the day was

_____

_____

My overall feeling and mood of the day was

_____

_____

I reduced my stress by

_____

_____

I am going to bed grateful for

_____

_____

Date   /   /

I woke up grateful for

_____

_____

The best part of my day was

_____

_____

My healthy habit of the day was

_____

_____

The healthy food I chose to nourish my body was

_____

_____

The amount of water I drank was

_____

_____

My active movement of the day was

_____

_____

My overall feeling and mood of the day was

_____

_____

I reduced my stress by

_____

_____

I am going to bed grateful for

_____

_____

Date   /   /

I woke up grateful for

_____

_____

The best part of my day was

_____

_____

My healthy habit of the day was

_____

_____

The healthy food I chose to nourish my body was

_____

_____

The amount of water I drank was

_____

_____

My active movement of the day was

_____

_____

My overall feeling and mood of the day was

_____

_____

I reduced my stress by

_____

_____

I am going to bed grateful for

_____

_____

Date   /   /

I woke up grateful for

_____

_____

The best part of my day was

_____

_____

My healthy habit of the day was

_____

_____

The healthy food I chose to nourish my body was

_____

_____

The amount of water I drank was

_____

_____

My active movement of the day was

_____

_____

My overall feeling and mood of the day was

_____

_____

I reduced my stress by

_____

_____

I am going to bed grateful for

_____

_____

Date   /   /

I woke up grateful for

_____

_____

The best part of my day was

_____

_____

My healthy habit of the day was

_____

_____

The healthy food I chose to nourish my body was

_____

_____

The amount of water I drank was

_____

_____

My active movement of the day was

_____

_____

My overall feeling and mood of the day was

_____

_____

I reduced my stress by

_____

_____

I am going to bed grateful for

_____

_____

Date   /   /

I woke up grateful for
_____
_____

The best part of my day was
_____
_____

My healthy habit of the day was
_____
_____

The healthy food I chose to nourish my body was
_____
_____

The amount of water I drank was
_____
_____

My active movement of the day was
_____
_____

My overall feeling and mood of the day was
_____
_____

I reduced my stress by
_____
_____

I am going to bed grateful for
_____
_____

Date   /   /

I woke up grateful for
_____
_____

The best part of my day was
_____
_____

My healthy habit of the day was
_____
_____

The healthy food I chose to nourish my body was
_____
_____

The amount of water I drank was
_____
_____

My active movement of the day was
_____
_____

My overall feeling and mood of the day was
_____
_____

I reduced my stress by
_____
_____

I am going to bed grateful for
_____
_____

Date   /   /

I woke up grateful for

_____

_____

The best part of my day was

_____

_____

My healthy habit of the day was

_____

_____

The healthy food I chose to nourish my body was

_____

_____

The amount of water I drank was

_____

_____

My active movement of the day was

_____

_____

My overall feeling and mood of the day was

_____

_____

I reduced my stress by

_____

_____

I am going to bed grateful for

_____

_____

Date / /

I woke up grateful for

_____

_____

The best part of my day was

_____

_____

My healthy habit of the day was

_____

_____

The healthy food I chose to nourish my body was

_____

_____

The amount of water I drank was

_____

_____

My active movement of the day was

_____

_____

My overall feeling and mood of the day was

_____

_____

I reduced my stress by

_____

_____

I am going to bed grateful for

_____

_____

Date / /

I woke up grateful for

_____

_____

The best part of my day was

_____

_____

My healthy habit of the day was

_____

_____

The healthy food I chose to nourish my body was

_____

_____

The amount of water I drank was

_____

_____

My active movement of the day was

_____

_____

My overall feeling and mood of the day was

_____

_____

I reduced my stress by

_____

_____

I am going to bed grateful for

_____

_____

Date   /   /

I woke up grateful for

_____

_____

The best part of my day was

_____

_____

My healthy habit of the day was

_____

_____

The healthy food I chose to nourish my body was

_____

_____

The amount of water I drank was

_____

_____

My active movement of the day was

_____

_____

My overall feeling and mood of the day was

_____

_____

I reduced my stress by

_____

_____

I am going to bed grateful for

_____

_____

Date   /   /

I woke up grateful for

_____

_____

The best part of my day was

_____

_____

My healthy habit of the day was

_____

_____

The healthy food I chose to nourish my body was

_____

_____

The amount of water I drank was

_____

_____

My active movement of the day was

_____

_____

My overall feeling and mood of the day was

_____

_____

I reduced my stress by

_____

_____

I am going to bed grateful for

_____

_____

Date / /

I woke up grateful for

_____

_____

The best part of my day was

_____

_____

My healthy habit of the day was

_____

_____

The healthy food I chose to nourish my body was

_____

_____

The amount of water I drank was

_____

_____

My active movement of the day was

_____

_____

My overall feeling and mood of the day was

_____

_____

I reduced my stress by

_____

_____

I am going to bed grateful for

_____

_____

Date   /   /

I woke up grateful for

_____

_____

The best part of my day was

_____

_____

My healthy habit of the day was

_____

_____

The healthy food I chose to nourish my body was

_____

_____

The amount of water I drank was

_____

_____

My active movement of the day was

_____

_____

My overall feeling and mood of the day was

_____

_____

I reduced my stress by

_____

_____

I am going to bed grateful for

_____

_____

Date   /   /

I woke up grateful for

_____

_____

The best part of my day was

_____

_____

My healthy habit of the day was

_____

_____

The healthy food I chose to nourish my body was

_____

_____

The amount of water I drank was

_____

_____

My active movement of the day was

_____

_____

My overall feeling and mood of the day was

_____

_____

I reduced my stress by

_____

_____

I am going to bed grateful for

_____

_____

Date / /

I woke up grateful for

_____

_____

The best part of my day was

_____

_____

My healthy habit of the day was

_____

_____

The healthy food I chose to nourish my body was

_____

_____

The amount of water I drank was

_____

_____

My active movement of the day was

_____

_____

My overall feeling and mood of the day was

_____

_____

I reduced my stress by

_____

_____

I am going to bed grateful for

_____

_____

Date   /   /

I woke up grateful for

_____

_____

The best part of my day was

_____

_____

My healthy habit of the day was

_____

_____

The healthy food I chose to nourish my body was

_____

_____

The amount of water I drank was

_____

_____

My active movement of the day was

_____

_____

My overall feeling and mood of the day was

_____

_____

I reduced my stress by

_____

_____

I am going to bed grateful for

_____

_____

MY HEALTHY LIFE JOURNAL

Date / /

I woke up grateful for
_____
_____

The best part of my day was
_____
_____

My healthy habit of the day was
_____
_____

The healthy food I chose to nourish my body was
_____
_____

The amount of water I drank was
_____
_____

My active movement of the day was
_____
_____

My overall feeling and mood of the day was
_____
_____

I reduced my stress by
_____
_____

I am going to bed grateful for
_____
_____

Date   /   /

I woke up grateful for

_____

_____

The best part of my day was

_____

_____

My healthy habit of the day was

_____

_____

The healthy food I chose to nourish my body was

_____

_____

The amount of water I drank was

_____

_____

My active movement of the day was

_____

_____

My overall feeling and mood of the day was

_____

_____

I reduced my stress by

_____

_____

I am going to bed grateful for

_____

_____

Date   /   /

I woke up grateful for
_____
_____

The best part of my day was
_____
_____

My healthy habit of the day was
_____
_____

The healthy food I chose to nourish my body was
_____
_____

The amount of water I drank was
_____
_____

My active movement of the day was
_____
_____

My overall feeling and mood of the day was
_____
_____

I reduced my stress by
_____
_____

I am going to bed grateful for
_____
_____

Date   /   /

I woke up grateful for
_____
_____

The best part of my day was
_____
_____

My healthy habit of the day was
_____
_____

The healthy food I chose to nourish my body was
_____
_____

The amount of water I drank was
_____
_____

My active movement of the day was
_____
_____

My overall feeling and mood of the day was
_____
_____

I reduced my stress by
_____
_____

I am going to bed grateful for
_____
_____

Date   /   /

I woke up grateful for

_____

_____

The best part of my day was

_____

_____

My healthy habit of the day was

_____

_____

The healthy food I chose to nourish my body was

_____

_____

The amount of water I drank was

_____

_____

My active movement of the day was

_____

_____

My overall feeling and mood of the day was

_____

_____

I reduced my stress by

_____

_____

I am going to bed grateful for

_____

_____

Date   /   /

I woke up grateful for

_____

_____

The best part of my day was

_____

_____

My healthy habit of the day was

_____

_____

The healthy food I chose to nourish my body was

_____

_____

The amount of water I drank was

_____

_____

My active movement of the day was

_____

_____

My overall feeling and mood of the day was

_____

_____

I reduced my stress by

_____

_____

I am going to bed grateful for

_____

_____

Date   /   /

I woke up grateful for
_____
_____

The best part of my day was
_____
_____

My healthy habit of the day was
_____
_____

The healthy food I chose to nourish my body was
_____
_____

The amount of water I drank was
_____
_____

My active movement of the day was
_____
_____

My overall feeling and mood of the day was
_____
_____

I reduced my stress by
_____
_____

I am going to bed grateful for
_____
_____

Date / /

I woke up grateful for

_____

_____

The best part of my day was

_____

_____

My healthy habit of the day was

_____

_____

The healthy food I chose to nourish my body was

_____

_____

The amount of water I drank was

_____

_____

My active movement of the day was

_____

_____

My overall feeling and mood of the day was

_____

_____

I reduced my stress by

_____

_____

I am going to bed grateful for

_____

_____

Date   /   /

I woke up grateful for

_____

_____

The best part of my day was

_____

_____

My healthy habit of the day was

_____

_____

The healthy food I chose to nourish my body was

_____

_____

The amount of water I drank was

_____

_____

My active movement of the day was

_____

_____

My overall feeling and mood of the day was

_____

_____

I reduced my stress by

_____

_____

I am going to bed grateful for

_____

_____

Date / /

I woke up grateful for

_____

The best part of my day was

_____

My healthy habit of the day was

_____

The healthy food I chose to nourish my body was

_____

The amount of water I drank was

_____

My active movement of the day was

_____

My overall feeling and mood of the day was

_____

I reduced my stress by

_____

I am going to bed grateful for

_____

_____

Date   /   /

I woke up grateful for
_____
_____

The best part of my day was
_____
_____

My healthy habit of the day was
_____
_____

The healthy food I chose to nourish my body was
_____
_____

The amount of water I drank was
_____
_____

My active movement of the day was
_____
_____

My overall feeling and mood of the day was
_____
_____

I reduced my stress by
_____
_____

I am going to bed grateful for
_____
_____

Date / /

I woke up grateful for

_____

_____

The best part of my day was

_____

_____

My healthy habit of the day was

_____

_____

The healthy food I chose to nourish my body was

_____

_____

The amount of water I drank was

_____

_____

My active movement of the day was

_____

_____

My overall feeling and mood of the day was

_____

_____

I reduced my stress by

_____

_____

I am going to bed grateful for

_____

_____

Date   /   /

I woke up grateful for

_____

_____

The best part of my day was

_____

_____

My healthy habit of the day was

_____

_____

The healthy food I chose to nourish my body was

_____

_____

The amount of water I drank was

_____

_____

My active movement of the day was

_____

_____

My overall feeling and mood of the day was

_____

_____

I reduced my stress by

_____

_____

I am going to bed grateful for

_____

_____

Date / /

I woke up grateful for

_____

_____

The best part of my day was

_____

_____

My healthy habit of the day was

_____

_____

The healthy food I chose to nourish my body was

_____

_____

The amount of water I drank was

_____

_____

My active movement of the day was

_____

_____

My overall feeling and mood of the day was

_____

_____

I reduced my stress by

_____

_____

I am going to bed grateful for

_____

_____

Date   /   /

I woke up grateful for

_____

_____

The best part of my day was

_____

_____

My healthy habit of the day was

_____

_____

The healthy food I chose to nourish my body was

_____

_____

The amount of water I drank was

_____

_____

My active movement of the day was

_____

_____

My overall feeling and mood of the day was

_____

_____

I reduced my stress by

_____

_____

I am going to bed grateful for

_____

_____

Date / /

I woke up grateful for
_____
_____

The best part of my day was
_____
_____

My healthy habit of the day was
_____
_____

The healthy food I chose to nourish my body was
_____
_____

The amount of water I drank was
_____
_____

My active movement of the day was
_____
_____

My overall feeling and mood of the day was
_____
_____

I reduced my stress by
_____
_____

I am going to bed grateful for
_____
_____

Date   /   /

I woke up grateful for

_____

_____

The best part of my day was

_____

_____

My healthy habit of the day was

_____

_____

The healthy food I chose to nourish my body was

_____

_____

The amount of water I drank was

_____

_____

My active movement of the day was

_____

_____

My overall feeling and mood of the day was

_____

_____

I reduced my stress by

_____

_____

I am going to bed grateful for

_____

_____

Date / /

I woke up grateful for
_____
_____

The best part of my day was
_____
_____

My healthy habit of the day was
_____
_____

The healthy food I chose to nourish my body was
_____
_____

The amount of water I drank was
_____
_____

My active movement of the day was
_____
_____

My overall feeling and mood of the day was
_____
_____

I reduced my stress by
_____
_____

I am going to bed grateful for
_____
_____

Date   /   /

I woke up grateful for

_____

_____

The best part of my day was

_____

_____

My healthy habit of the day was

_____

_____

The healthy food I chose to nourish my body was

_____

_____

The amount of water I drank was

_____

_____

My active movement of the day was

_____

_____

My overall feeling and mood of the day was

_____

_____

I reduced my stress by

_____

_____

I am going to bed grateful for

_____

_____

Date   / /

I woke up grateful for

_____

_____

The best part of my day was

_____

_____

My healthy habit of the day was

_____

_____

The healthy food I chose to nourish my body was

_____

_____

The amount of water I drank was

_____

_____

My active movement of the day was

_____

_____

My overall feeling and mood of the day was

_____

_____

I reduced my stress by

_____

_____

I am going to bed grateful for

_____

_____

Date   /   /

I woke up grateful for

_____

_____

The best part of my day was

_____

_____

My healthy habit of the day was

_____

_____

The healthy food I chose to nourish my body was

_____

_____

The amount of water I drank was

_____

_____

My active movement of the day was

_____

_____

My overall feeling and mood of the day was

_____

_____

I reduced my stress by

_____

_____

I am going to bed grateful for

_____

_____

Date   /   /

I woke up grateful for

_____

_____

The best part of my day was

_____

_____

My healthy habit of the day was

_____

_____

The healthy food I chose to nourish my body was

_____

_____

The amount of water I drank was

_____

_____

My active movement of the day was

_____

_____

My overall feeling and mood of the day was

_____

_____

I reduced my stress by

_____

_____

I am going to bed grateful for

_____

_____

Date   /   /

I woke up grateful for
_____
_____

The best part of my day was
_____
_____

My healthy habit of the day was
_____
_____

The healthy food I chose to nourish my body was
_____
_____

The amount of water I drank was
_____
_____

My active movement of the day was
_____
_____

My overall feeling and mood of the day was
_____
_____

I reduced my stress by
_____
_____

I am going to bed grateful for
_____
_____

Date   /   /

I woke up grateful for

_____

_____

The best part of my day was

_____

_____

My healthy habit of the day was

_____

_____

The healthy food I chose to nourish my body was

_____

_____

The amount of water I drank was

_____

_____

My active movement of the day was

_____

_____

My overall feeling and mood of the day was

_____

_____

I reduced my stress by

_____

_____

I am going to bed grateful for

_____

_____

Date / /

I woke up grateful for
_____
_____

The best part of my day was
_____
_____

My healthy habit of the day was
_____
_____

The healthy food I chose to nourish my body was
_____
_____

The amount of water I drank was
_____
_____

My active movement of the day was
_____
_____

My overall feeling and mood of the day was
_____
_____

I reduced my stress by
_____
_____

I am going to bed grateful for
_____
_____

Date / /

I woke up grateful for

_____

_____

The best part of my day was

_____

_____

My healthy habit of the day was

_____

_____

The healthy food I chose to nourish my body was

_____

_____

The amount of water I drank was

_____

_____

My active movement of the day was

_____

_____

My overall feeling and mood of the day was

_____

_____

I reduced my stress by

_____

_____

I am going to bed grateful for

_____

_____

Date   /   /

I woke up grateful for

_____

_____

The best part of my day was

_____

_____

My healthy habit of the day was

_____

_____

The healthy food I chose to nourish my body was

_____

_____

The amount of water I drank was

_____

_____

My active movement of the day was

_____

_____

My overall feeling and mood of the day was

_____

_____

I reduced my stress by

_____

_____

I am going to bed grateful for

_____

_____

Notes

Notes

Notes

Notes

Notes

Notes

Notes

Notes

Notes

Notes

Notes

Notes

Made in the USA
Columbia, SC
22 July 2020

13474459R00162